INSTANT
WINNER

ALSO BY CARRIE FOUNTAIN

Burn Lake

INSTANT WINNER

CARRIE FOUNTAIN

PENGUIN POETS

PENGUIN BOOKS
Published by the Penguin Group
Penguin Group (USA) LLC,
375 Hudson Street,
New York, New York 10014

USA | Canada | UK | Ireland | Australia | New Zealand | India | South Africa | China
penguin.com
A Penguin Random House Company

First published in Penguin Books 2014

LIBRARY OF CONGRESS CATALOGING-IN-PUBLICATION DATA
Fountain, Carrie.
[Poems. Selections]
Instant winner / Carrie Fountain.
pages cm.—(Penguin Poets)
Summary: "A moving, authentic exploration of spirituality and the domestic from a
prize-winning poet. The wry, supple poems in Carrie Fountain's second collection take
the form of prayers and meditations chronicling the existential shifts brought on by
parenthood, spiritual searching, and the profound, often beguiling experience of being a
self, inside a body, with a soul. Fountain's voice is at once deep and loose, enacting the
dawning of spiritual insight, but without leaving the daily world, matching the feeling of
the "pure holiness in motherhood" with the "thuds the giant dumpsters make behind the
strip mall when they're tossed back to the pavement by the trash truck." In these wise,
accessible, deeply emotional poems, she captures a contemporary longing for spiritual
meaning that's wary of prepackaged wisdom-a longing answered most fully by attending
to the hustle and bustle of everyday life"—Provided by publisher.
ISBN 978-0-14-312663-8 (paperback)
I. Title.
PS3606.O84425A6 2014
811'6—dc23   2014014461

Printed in the United States of America
1   3   5   7   9   10   8   6   4   2

Set in Warnock Light Display
Designed by Ginger Legato

For my husband
and for our children

For, since I left Russia, I have not known with such great con-
viction that prayer and its time and its reverent and uncurtailed
gestures are the condition of God and of his return to those
who barely expect it and merely kneel down and stand up
again and are suddenly filled to the brim. . . .

—Rilke

CONTENTS

III

IV

ACKNOWLEDGMENTS

Some of these poems were first published in the following journals, to whose editors grateful acknowledgment is made:

The American Poetry Review

Bat City Review

Better

Ecotone

The Harlequin

Huizache: The Magazine of Latino Literature

Iron Horse Literary Review

The Journal

Southwestern American Literature

The Texas Observer

Tin House

Tupelo Quarterly

"Lazarus Dies Again" also appears in the anthology *New America: Contemporary Literature for a Changing Society,* edited by Holly Messitt and James Tolan and published by Autumn House Press in 2012.

Thanks to friends who read this book and gave me useful feedback and encouragement, especially Richard Robichaux, Phil Pardi, Beth Eakman, and Margo Rabb. Thanks to Emily Forland for her keen advice and friendship. Endless thanks to Paul Slovak at Penguin. For mentorship that began when I was very young, I am tremendously grateful to Mark Medoff. Thanks to Jim Magnuson, one of the few famous writers I have known. The Michener Center for Writers still feels like home—thanks for letting O bounce on the furniture there when we come by. Thanks to Tony Hoagland, who continues to teach me. I would do very little without the ongoing encouragement and advice I receive in my abiding friendship with Naomi Shihab Nye.

Greatest thanks of all to my husband, Kirk Lynn, who has given me so much—so many blessings, including our children, O and J—and who helps me live a life like his, *filled to the brim.*

INSTANT
WINNER

I

POEM WITHOUT NEW YEAR'S RESOLUTIONS

Maybe it's no longer a pure kind of behavior
you seek, with so much breathing in it

and so much regret. What if you take with you
only this dark morning and the insane thuds

the giant dumpsters make behind the strip mall
when they're tossed back to the pavement

by the trash truck? Let Spanish go, let running
go, let yoga do flawless back walkovers across

the dead lawn in its very flattering leotard,
let it just be gone. Let this body

be the body you'll carry forward, at least
into this day. Let the sound of the dumpsters

wake the baby so she starts calling for you
too early, *Come upping me right now!*

in her new businessy voice. What if this is just
your luck and all you need to do is let it

come into the room—just let it come—let it
take off its coat and talk to a few people

before you reach for its elbow, kiss its cheek,
and start telling it what it owes you?

PRAYER (EASY)

Who is running this
lonely operation? A wall

of switches, a hall
leading out into

another hall. Every time
you turn on the hair dryer,

the lights go out.
So easy to feel dread—easy

to feel anything, really.
What I'm seeking is only

partially emotion. God, I can
picture it perfectly in my mind,

though I have no recollection
of ever having seen it.

THE PARABLE OF THE TALENTS

The man in the pig suit is back,
standing outside the gates

of the state capitol, holding a sign
that reads LAWYERS ARE SWINE,

his bitter face only just visible
inside the soiled pink vinyl, his outrage

clambering over westbound traffic
on Eleventh. It's so heavy, believing

there is a story in every moment, every
person, all those spots you press

to find they're rotted straight through,
all those ropes of thickened

scar tissue—the divorce gone bad,
the drunk driver gone free; it's always

complicated, even when the message
is *fuck it*. He makes me think

of Susan, beginning to cry, asking,
Who do you think Jesus will come to first,

if not the insane and the depraved?
See, that was a complicated moment

for me, as my jealousy of Susan's faith
was exactly equal to my jealousy

of the insane and depraved to whom Jesus
would come. The light stays red long after

I expect it to turn green, so I watch
the cars as they turn south

on Congress, as they go on with
their lives. In the backseat, the baby

is silent. No words yet, not a single
word, only sounds. She is pure

of story, sitting, facing backward,
looking up, maybe, to the rotunda,

where the great woman of Texas stands
all day and night in her robe with her arm

extended elegantly toward heaven,
holding that one big star above her head.

Strange woman. I read somewhere that
to make her recognizable from this far

her features had to be exaggerated
beyond recognition and that close up

she looks like a monster.

WORKING MOTHER POEM

All I want to do is go home
and take off these pants
and make Tuscan bean soup,
carefully following the recipe
stained darkly with soups
of the past, dicing celery
with the news on while the baby
sits balanced on her
outrageous thighs and plays
Making Tuscan Bean Soup,
which involves pouring all
the tea bags out of their boxes
and into the giant pot I will
eventually have to squat down
and take away from her.
When I do, she will cry,
and her crying face will be
a house with its garage door
rolling open at four a.m.,
flooding the dark street
with fluorescent light.
When I apologize to my daughter
it won't be like the apologies
of my past.

IN THE DISTANT PAST

Things weren't very specific
when I was in labor,

yet everything was
there, suddenly: all that

my body had known,
even things I'd only been

reminded of occasionally,
as when a stranger's scent

had reminded me
of someone I'd known

in the distant past. The few
men I'd loved but didn't

marry. The time, living
alone in Albuquerque,

when I fainted in the kitchen
one morning before work

and woke up on the floor,
covered in coffee. Finally.

it was coming. It was all moving
forward. Finally, it was all going

to pass through me. It was
beginning to happen

and it was all going to happen
in one single night.

No more lingering
in the adolescent pools

of memory, no more giving it
a little more time to see

if things would get better
or worse. No more moving

from one place to the next.
Finally, my body was all

that had ever been given
to me, it was all I had,

and I sweated through it
in layers, so that when,

in the end, I was finally
standing outside myself

and watching, I could see
that what brought me

into the world was pulling
you into the world,

and I could see that my body
was giving you up

and giving you to me,
and where in my body

there were talents, there
were talents, and where

there were no talents,
there would be scars.

NOSTALGIA SAYS NO

Your father is a man with a mustache
and black hair sitting on his haunches
in the sunlight unhooking warm cans of beer
from a six-pack and forcing each
with an easy shove into the white heart
of the ice chest. But no, that was
years ago. Where is the crunching sound
the ice makes? Where is the slow melt
of the passing day, the dead center
of the birthday party, the piñata swaying
heavily overhead? And the now-dead
with their hands folded and their legs
crossed in their lawn chairs—when did they
stand and walk out of the yard, oblivious,
saying, *Save me a piece of cake*, saying, *No,*
I'll be back, save me a piece of cake?
Is it really that easy? Remind me:
oblivious is a word with no eyes or hands.
It can't get far on its own, right?

A DREAM OF THE BAD CHILDHOOD

I pulled the geranium up by its reedy neck
out of the pot where it sat in the window
all those years, facing the highway. It gave
so easily, cleanly, a sick bulk of white roots
grown back up over themselves again and again
where they'd wanted to go down, into
the good earth, into the deeper dark.

SURPRISE

I don't want to teach you anything
or show you my wound or have you taste
the amazing thing I made this morning
with only what we had left in the fridge
before you came home with new groceries.
I'm as tired as you are of genius. Hey,
do you know where we put the sky?
I haven't seen it for months.
When I was in New Mexico last week
all I did was push the baby in her stroller
and worry about the sun on her legs
and think about coming home. Now
I'm home and I'm thinking of the way
the light came in off the runway
while I was waiting in the airport
for the return flight, feeding the baby
a hundred Cheerios, one by one, thinking,
I don't even know how to visit New Mexico
anymore, thinking, I guess there isn't going to be
a time when I live like I lived that summer
in Santa Fe, that summer-into-fall
I've for so long told myself I will someday
return to, that place I've kept, that ace
in the hole, that life with mornings
and afternoons that I am still holding back
with the very tip of my fingernail. After all,
this afternoon is the afternoon I've been
waiting for all my life: running
the vacuum over the rugs while you walk

the baby around the block and my breasts
heat and tingle as they fill again with milk
and someone with the wrong number
calls my cell again and again, refusing
to take *there is no Phillip here* for an answer.
This is, after all, the exact life I take with me
to bed each night, digging deeper and deeper
into its blood-dark soil, waking some mornings
from dreams that shake me and leave me
with a thirst for the past or the future,
a distance I can never reach—dreams
of a house I don't recognize but know
I have lived in all my life, someone
I've never seen saying, *Reach under
your shoulder blade and feel with your fingers
the place where I pierced you.* Oh,
that summer: Why did I have to leave it
cracked open behind me as I went? How
did I even do that? How did I get that
one sky to stay wedged there, blue as the sky
and just as big?

FOUR MONTHS OLD

All the baby knows
is the flop of her limbs

and the milky blue vein
of sleep and the parking lot

of her animal fear,
the cars left there overnight,

windshields dark and thick
with dew. The rest is

completely unknown,
the complete darkness

of her white room,
where she sleeps

on a clean sheet
printed with baby

crocodiles and lions
wearing diapers.

EATING THE AVOCADO

Now I know that I've never described
anything, not one single thing, not
the flesh of the avocado which darkens
so quickly, though if you scrape
what's been exposed to the air it's new-green
beneath like nothing ever happened.
I want to describe this evening, though
it's not spectacular. The baby babbling
in the other room over the din
and whistle of a football game, and now
the dog just outside the door, scratching,
rattling the tags on her collar, the car
going by, far away but loud, a car without
a muffler, and the sound of the baby
returning again, pleasure and weight.
I want to describe the baby. I want to describe
the baby for many hours to anyone
who wishes to hear me. My feelings for her
take me so far inside myself I can see the pure
holiness in motherhood, and it makes me
burn with success and fear, the hole her
coming has left open, widening. Last night
we fed her some of the avocado I've just
finished eating while writing this poem.
Her first food. I thought my heart might burst,
knowing she would no longer be made
entirely of me, flesh of my flesh. Startled

in her amusing way by the idea of eating,
she tried to take it in, but her mouth
pushed it out. And my heart did burst.

PRAYER (RINSED)

By now I feel rinsed
by time, by what

can happen and what can't
happen; rinsed too

by surprise, by the accident
and then the discipline

of love, the body
I've come to, which I am,

even now, leaving behind,
and the mind, the weird

guilt of the passing hour,
the shame of clocks, the way

the day opens its wet blue
petals, then whitens

in the center and falls off
heavily into night; rinsed,

even, by the conversation
I'm having with myself

right now, waiting for the next part
of this sentence, for the next

airplane to pass overhead,
above the city, through

the equanimity of sky, making
that sickening sound of force

and action that is simply
the sound of this prayer

being made and this prayer
being torn apart again.

I WISH I HAD A GURU

I want a bad one, the kind
who takes all the measly particulars
of life and works them

into one simple, messed-up thing:
a wad of gum a child is forced to spit
into her mother's upturned palm

before entering the public library,
a cloud, far off, emitting a song
you can almost place, but can't

place. *Was that song playing*
the night I drove myself
to the emergency room?

I wish I could be brainwashed,
because brainwashing
sounds great, like the feeling

you get when you stand up
too quickly and sense
you're going to faint

but know in the same instant
that you're not
going to faint. That feeling:

like standing
next to yourself, like starting
all over again in white, legs

shaved, hair cleanly parted,
like *sound check, one two, one two,*
until your soiled, crying life

sees you through the crowd
and rushes to you, reaching you
just as you're pushing through

the emergency exit, just as
the alarm bells go off stingingly,
grabbing hold of your thigh,

claiming you, so that you
understand suddenly
and only for an instant

that you are one being inside
one body: sealed, exquisite,
animate; that you

were made from others
and came from a far, unseeable
place, a source

that can not be traced;
and that you will continue
to take what you are handed

and run—you will run
as far and as fast as you can
with whatever breath

you have, right up until the end.
That feeling: it's like sliding
your two hands

beneath the whole
frosted cake of your life,
lifting it carefully

from the platter and shoving it
into your face, the whole time saying,
Oh, now this is a really bad idea.

PRAYER (SNAP)

So many things that mean
nothing, though I can't

think of one off the top of my head.
Movement in the bushes,

a breezy April morning, the last
full week we'll spend in this,

our first house. Though
we're leaving, I keep it neat

and clean, counters wiped, floors
swept, a pile of boxes in the corner.

We inch along, accumulating
and losing, grabbing for and

pushing away, straightening up
and then taking down. At any moment

something very close—within arm's
reach—could signify everything.

As a girl, I spoke to God
because I believed God could

hear me. Always problems, impossible
situations, always something

to ask for. What a talent! Now
I so rarely lift my prayers. What

am I waiting for? A snap, a fall,
a branch coming down, breaking

another, the both of them finally
falling into the bushes, this life suddenly

set in motion by that one. Or is this
the snap? Right here. Or is this it?

SELLING THE HOUSE

This room—pale yellow walls—where my husband once delivered
a love note by tucking it beneath her collar, then asking me to call the dog.

That corner in the living room where I read every morning in the dark
for an hour and a half one winter until I finished *War and Peace.* The morning

I finished it, I looked up from Tolstoy's last metaphor to see it was already light
outside and nothing would ever be the same. The nick in the back door I made

when I kicked it. The lawn we killed and grew halfway again. And the stories
Deborah across the street told about the man who lived here before us,

who'd been a prisoner of war and had been so careful about the lawn, going out
mornings with a pair of kitchen scissors to trim along the

curb. The light in the windows, the toilet's stupid grin, the worst fights
and the best. It is a small price. This could be yours.

IT'S NOTHING

It's not the instantaneous disappearance
of the mailman after he dumps the mail
into the box. It's not the smoke detector's
wide, dead eye. It's not this weird pain
in my shoulder. I don't think it's something
that can be caused by sleeping in the wrong
position. Nor is it the man in my dream
last night, the stranger wearing a ball cap
who followed me through the department
store of my youth, the store downtown
called the Popular, where my grandmother
bought her impeccable slacks, creased like
extreme sanity. Every time I looked, the man
was closer. I woke after I realized, in the dream,
that there was no use trying to evade him.
He'd catch me eventually. It wouldn't matter
if we were in the shoe department or in
housewares. But oh, how slowly he was
catching me. I woke at four a.m. and stayed
awake. Now, every time I look out the window
it's brighter out there, though I can hardly
believe time is passing at all.

IN THE FIRST YEAR OF MARRIAGE

Kirk calls. The dog begs
for something; I don't know what.

This is back when I have that job
so awful I can feel it on the weekends

waiting across town for Monday
so it can be awful again in real time.

This is back when Kirk is in Boston
for weeks at a time, working. He calls

in the evening and we talk about
our days and things in the news,

and then, when we have nothing more
to say, we hang up, though tonight,

just after we do, I remember that
I'd wanted to tell him that earlier,

trolling the parking lot at the grocery
store, looking for a spot, I watched

a woman get into her parked car
and then sit there, putting on lipstick,

then blush, and then just sit there
doing nothing in her silver Corolla

while I waited under my dark cloud
for her space, which I'd already begun

to think of as my own, and that
eventually I had to pull forward, I had to

give up on that life, and the only spot
left open was out where there weren't

any light posts, out where the dark
was invented, where the man

sitting in his car in the space
next to mine didn't have

a face—he didn't have a face—and oh,
then I longed for my husband.

INSTANT WINNER

Great, I've been wanting for a while to live
my real life again, driving to work each morning
seeing the billboards growing up so fast—the egg
sandwich dripping its triangles of cheese, the beer
bottle sweating heavily under blue lights—seeing
that the city has suddenly been built up on both sides
right to the very lip of the interstate; I've been
wanting to live my life again as I switch lanes
in the whir at the very center of traffic; I've been
wanting to live my life again, stepping into
the parking lot, stopping at Target for bananas
and diapers, diapers and trash bags, diapers
and ibuprofen, walking from classroom
to office, office to meeting, my phone
in my pocket, always ready—always ready for
my real life to call, to say, *Is this Carrie Fountain?*
to say, *I found you, finally, and I have some big news.*

THIRTY-SIXTH BIRTHDAY SONNET

The dove hit my office window and died,
leaving a perfect silhouette in dust
and down and fat flecks of bright red blood.
Weeks later, I'm still confronting this death.
Much earlier in the evening, I wrote
thank you on my palms and Kirk took a photo
for Michael, who got us the tickets. But
now it's much later and the ink won't
come off. And so I keep confronting
my gratitude. Kirk says, *Look, it's your*
birthday for exactly one more hour, before
he falls asleep. My face in the mirror
says, *By now, I have had over five weeks*
of birthdays. Still, I want more, more.

INSTINCT

What is it about certain other dogs that makes her
bare her curved white teeth and explode at the end of her leash
while we're out for a walk through this same old neighborhood

with its not-surprising bends, its lawns and strewn recycling bins—
this sweet, matronly animal who has just now elongated her
comically thin body, lying wide open in front of the window,

waiting with me for the morning to bear fruit? I think
her entire world must begin and end every five minutes. How easy
it is to become envious of every single thing you're not.

POEM WITHOUT SLEEP

All the things that could happen
to the baby came to me last night

as I was falling asleep. Children
of mine, they climbed into bed, sweaty

and whimpering in colorful pajamas,
with their stories, which were sad,

and their fears, which were crystalline.
Each time another arrived

I'd think, OK, that's got to be it.
But then another would push through

with her forehead or elbow, her
hot breath saying *Mama,* saying

Mama, please. Soon there were so many
I couldn't see any one of them,

I couldn't hear their distinct voices,
and they jumped on the bed,

on my chest, on my face, until it was
all black with a white flash

and a thick, electric ringing in the ears.
And now, here's the morning.

Here's the tree flickering
behind the shade, dumb tree

with its one arm raised to the sky.
Here's the silent tipping into another day.

And now, finally, finally, the baby, blowing
her famous raspberries down the dark

static hallway of the baby monitor. And now
she begins to whimper. And now she cries out.

And here I go to her, thank God.
Here I go to help her little life.

PRAYER (IMPOSSIBLE)

I don't care how much time
I've wasted. And I don't care how much

time I will waste in the future, looking
at photographs, listening for summer

thunder and wondering if my daughter
can hear it in her classroom

across town, where she is likely eating
a snack at the spot at the table labeled

with her name. All of it—even
the absence, the great and constant

absence, the accumulating absences
and the fleeting ones, too—I don't care

anymore how easy it looks, or how
impossible. I'm counting all of it.

THE STORY ABOUT THE BIRDS CHANGES
AFTER THE BABY IS BORN

Why have I held on to it so tightly, gripping
its thin wrist, dragging it behind me all these

years, *Hurry up*? It was summertime in the desert—
inarticulate summertime—and the boys

were popping grackles off a wire with their BB guns.
The ones they didn't hit kept coming back, shaking

the heat out of their feathers and looking around
with their unwieldy eyes. *Stupid birds* is what

the one boy said. Because I was watching them,
he'd turn every once in a while and point his gun

at me, and the other boys would laugh, not knowing
what to do. He was having a bad childhood, but

who wasn't? I didn't fly away. I stayed where I was.
But I wanted to go. In the story, that had always

been enough. But it's not enough anymore.
So I'm giving this story away.

PERSONAL WATERMELON

Please don't touch it. It's mine. It's
personal. The juices are secrets
I have been keeping from myself, even

from myself. It's everything, really. Every
time I check my e-mail the watermelon
still hasn't sent me the notification

of my great and imminent success, and that
really bothers me. What kind of bedtime
story is my husband telling my daughter

anyway? Now the two of them are howling
like wolves. Oh, how I envy her off-switch
sleep. How is it the thing I'm most proud of

is that I know my pride well and have taught it
to do tricks? What is holy—that's all I want to know.
Here's a heart with juice and seeds. It's mine.

BUT THEN

Who knows why we bought the pair of lovebirds
we kept in the kitchen window, small and plump
as strawberries, peepish, astute, perched on the plastic

branch, preening each other with yellow beaks.
Two weeks and I hated everything about them: the crap
and the racket and the god-awful task of pouring out

the teaspoon of dirty water from the tiny dish
and filling it again from the tap, and the shame that came
from looking into the trap that was their cage and knowing

we'd put them there, we'd driven to the pet store
and singled them out to be caught with a gloved hand and paid for
with money. I think you hated them, too, though

for obvious reasons neither of us could say it. So long ago
now, all I really remember is the afternoon I was cleaning their cage
on the porch while a huge pink thunderstorm rolled over

the mesa, a mile of breeze preceding it, and I inadvertently lifted
the wire mesh from its base and released them—suddenly—one rising
and then the other, drawn upward like kites into the sky.

I scrambled to catch them and couldn't catch them and within seconds
they were gone forever, never to be seen or heard from again. Oh God,
I hated watching them struggle stupidly into the air, becoming more

and more free every second. But then, moments later, the porch
was silent, and I was surprised when I didn't feel a thing, only
the breeze in my face, new, oncoming, like the whole life I didn't know

I still had ahead of me. Later, I'd show you the empty cage
and whatever one-boned animal we'd made together
would snap dully between us. Within a week we'd be prepared

to never see each other again. Of course, the birds wouldn't make it.
I called and asked the guy at the pet store. Was there anything
I could do? *Oh, no way, ma'am,* he said, *those little things?*

PRAYER (*STOP IT*)

When I said I wanted to work harder than
everyone, I didn't mean work harder. I didn't

mean that I wanted to answer more e-mails
and forget to eat lunch. I meant sweat.

And I didn't mean sweat, of course, but light.
I guess I meant I wanted to shine brighter

than everyone. And that's where I've gone
wrong again and again. With or without

God, this moment continues to end and end.
With or without virtue. In the park yesterday,

sitting on the lawn with the baby, I watched
a boy and his younger sister walk to the pool.

He was carrying a bag with their towels;
she was wearing green floaties pushed

very high up on her arms. Once they'd passed,
the boy turned to the girl and yelled

Stop it! into her round face, and the girl
smiled hugely at having worn him down

and then assured him that she would
stop, and though I'd been watching them

and continued to watch them, I could not perceive
what it was she'd stopped doing.

PRAYER (CLOSE)

All morning it has stayed close, a cat with that
avid desire to be scratched roughly around the face and neck.

Choose me, it keeps saying. There's the dove's call—the very
sound of childhood, the very signal of spring. All morning

it has stayed close, and still I cannot touch it.

SUBURBAN SPRING

Last night it was the sage bush opening
its young purple fists; this morning
it was the slender mechanic

saying "your catalytic converter"
with his fat mouth, saying "pretty
pricey to replace it, ma'am."

I thought, Oh, see, he's playing a game
calling me ma'am, because I wanted
to think he was playing a game, though now,

only a few hours later, I'm one hundred
percent sure he wasn't playing a game.
Oh, earth, I'm an animal

again. Earth, I am born.
It's spring and bees are thrusting
their sugar-fat bodies into my elderly neighbor's

cherry blossoms while he sits
at the cool center of his yard, a stone
in a hat, repotting a sinewy geranium,

while my husband sits on the floor
in the living room, his back to the sofa, watching
a basketball game, the irregular squeak

of shoes on the court above the crowd's
unbent enthusiasm, his soft, clean penis—easy
to start, old friend, old enemy—asleep

in the warm, dark office of his crotch.
By now the young mechanic is stuck in traffic
on the way home, sitting

on a towel, protecting the leather
upholstery of the truck he can't afford
from the grime he collects

throughout the day, worrying
about money. I'm worrying about money,
too, but I'm always

worrying about money. Even
now—even right now, as the bees,
unaware of the age of the earth, unaware

of its size and its cruel and costly
turning, go about their business. It's all
the same for them. Oh, the cheap

motors of their bodies: they run
on desire, all day long, all day long, all
they do is make the world come back.

MEMORY OF THE PREGNANT BODY

It's abstract, strange, something on loan, something you've borrowed
from a friend. *I keep forgetting to give this back to you.* And then

it grows and comes until you can't give it back, because now it's yours,
or it's not yours, but it's yours. Glorious and terrifying

as cactus. Tender everything. There on a plane, there while teaching
class, reaching for a glass, there while sitting in traffic listening

to the call-in psychologist say in an exasperated way, "Listen, I'm
not a lawyer." It gets bigger, and then it opens. And then it disappears.

LAZARUS DIES AGAIN

He'd lived so long sometimes
it felt as if he'd taken someone else's life.
At night, his knees ached. And he still
thought about it all the time: how he'd been
a strange favorite once, how once
his eyes had been slit open like fruits
and he'd seen his tomb and he'd smelled
his powder-sweet life sifting back
through the obscure loam of his death.
What a day! His sisters weeping,
touching him, asking questions.
After a while he returned to his life,
resumed his labor. The tomb was sealed.
And eventually no one spoke of that time.
His sisters grew old and died.
Now, it was raining. It had been raining
for days. He'd been holding on
to a particular memory, something he'd seen
as a boy: a donkey in a pasture, far off,
waste steaming in the cold morning.
There were still things he dreaded.
Somehow he was amazed by that.
Now something began to slip. He breathed
and stopped breathing—and there
it was, once again—flickering at the edge
of the landscape—all this time, waiting
for him. That old flame. That dazzling end.
All this time he'd been waiting for it.
Still, it was nothing like he'd imagined it'd be.

HOTTEST SUMMER ON RECORD

for Susannah Benson

I'm thinking again about the night
we should've died:

fifteen, in the backseat
of an egg-shaped car

as those feral boys
started yelling *Balls out*

to the driver, who gripped
the wheel and locked

his elbows and drove faster
and faster until it felt

like there was nothing between us
and the end

but the soft shoulder
of the road, the constellations

of mosquitoes over the ditch,
the night reflected

in the still water there, murky
with pesticides,

then less, just flesh
on metal, metal on air,

then less, until it felt like
we could die

of speed alone, evaporate—
poof—sucked back into the holes

our insignificant histories
had made in the earth,

so that no one would ever
find a trace of us, not a spot

of blood or a point of impact,
no dust or smoke

or skid marks. Maybe then
we'd never have existed

at all. Oh, how many
times did I take my dumb life

in my hands and shove it
down deep between

my thighs so no one would
see it? And how many times

did I give it away, push it
over, baring everything,

daring the night to take it
away? Hard to tell

how many real deaths
we escaped to make it

to tonight, talking
on the phone while I sit

on the porch with the baby
asleep in my arms,

watching the dog chase the cat
then—surprise—they

switch, so that now the cat's
chasing the dog and, oh,

he's gaining on her.

PRAYER (STRANGER)

Driving to work this morning I saw the cat

in someone else's front yard, four or five houses
down, living a different life: a stranger, perfectly

civilized, whitish paws aligned, guarding their car,
watching me pass with not too much interest.

PRAYER (WILD)

A bunch of ducks out there on the lake
flaunting their indifference

to the choppy water, to this life
and the next, rocking woodenly, tooth-

white beaks, black eyes. Why do these
ducks make my soul go nuts

inside the responsibility of my body,
throwing itself at the beauty of the world

like a wild dog someone found
in the woods and took home

and fell in love with and chained
to the porch?

POEM SAYING NO

You become conspicuous.
A semitruck engine turns over
in the silent parking lot

of your chest. Out of the corner
of your eye you notice
before he does that the stranger

seated next to you has begun
to bleed from the nose.
You begin to smell like meat,

something that will expire. But
just wait. Just wait. They'll get
someone else to do it.

STUPID

Oh, it's a crude
little weapon, a spike,
a nail, and they
use it all day long—
all day long—to mean
anything
they want it to mean.
They're learning how
to hate, how it can be
so easy and pleasing,
like watching
a watermelon dropped
from a high rooftop
smash open
on the pavement below
over and over again
in slow motion
on a TV with the sound
turned down. I already
know how to hate. All
I want to say to them
is, Wait.

NEW YEAR'S MORNING

In my dream last night I took off
my hands—first the right, then

the left—the way I'd take off
a pair of gloves, and set them

in the dish where I sometimes
leave my keys. It was dim,

the dream, and there were reasons
for everything that happened,

motives I can't remember now,
though truly I long to do so,

as they could, of course, explain
so much. Outside, on the lawn,

the first newspaper of the year
lies limp in its plastic blue sack.

Someone was out this morning
before any of us, tossing papers

while we slept. It was probably
three o'clock when he peeled out

of bed, dressed, warmed up the car,
and left his wife under the covers,

she who hasn't even rolled over yet
to reach for him, never waking.

PRAYER (FAR AWAY)

You can stay behind the curtain
of the sky, far away, the farthest
thing away from me, and you can
promise that you'll never return
to this planet, to this galaxy. I don't
believe you. There are too many
moments: the public library
of my childhood, with its bleach-
over-urine smell; the taste of
swimming pools. Even those two
doves out there, sitting in the high
branches of that leaf-empty pecan—
even they know. They know the weight
of their feathers and feet. Now
they're gone. I'll never see them again.
But that doesn't mean I'll never see
them again.

IV

LIVABILITY

Behind the window out there, the AC unit
is whirring into this brand-new Saturday afternoon,

while in here, in this room, I've opened all the shades
to let the light in. A month ago my body

split and you appeared, wailing, wailing. I could
sail off into the pink sunset in that car insurance

commercial, wholly unafraid of my life,
now that you're here.

TWO WEEKS LATER, THE DOG RETURNS

All that time we were sleeping and waking, waking and driving
to work, turning off the iron, then going back after a few minutes

and unplugging it just to make sure. Her black eyes are full
of the same worry, the same apology, as she circles her bed,

as she falls casually into the space her body has made over years,
which is her destiny. Again it comes to me: how the living

body can feel irrevocable, like a church, cool and well lighted, a high
ceiling painted with tiny yellow stars.

PRAYER (THE LEDGE)

You think it's in the skull,
behind the eyes, a room

you make and then walk into.
You think it's the feeling

of desperate thirst
that sometimes arises

after you've begun to drink
deeply, when it's only ever been

the feeling you got
when finally, after many weeks

of staring at the impeccable
outline the dove's body left

when it crashed into your office
window, open-winged, and died,

you hung your ass
over the ledge and wiped it

away with a damp
Kleenex: the completion

of a perfect and miserable task.
Most often there is nothing—

really nothing—and the whole thing
feels like an idea you gave yourself,

like hypochondria, or, even more
distant, the memory of hypochondria,

and even that idea is a place
you can't be right now, because right now

you are in the car, waiting out
the endless light at the corner

of MLK and Congress, when the baby
suddenly says, *Song Mommy song now.*

YES

I am done smoking cigarettes, done waiting tables, done counting tips
at two a.m. in the neon-dark dance hall, done sleeping with young men
in my apartment, done facing them or not, thinking of oblivion, which
is better than nothing. I am done not wearing underwear because
it's so Victorian. I am done telling men I don't wear underwear because
it's so Victorian. I am done with the night a guy spread my legs
on a pool table, all those balls piled up in the pockets. I am done.
I am never going back. When I see that night on the street I will
drive past and never even glance over. I am done going to grad school,
nodding in your workshop. I am done teaching English as a second
language, saying *I* pointing to my chest, saying *you* pointing to them.
I am done teaching the poetry class where no one talked and no one
listened to me and outside the window the cottonwood wagged
its sun-white leaves in the breeze as if to say, *I give up, I give up.* I am done
being a childless woman, a childless wife, a woman with no scars
on her body. I am done with the wide afternoons of before, the long
stare, the tightly closed door. And I am done, too, for the most part,
with the daydream of after. I am after for now. I am turning up the heater
to see if that will make the baby sleep another fifteen minutes
so I can finish this poem. I am done thinking of the past as if it had
survived, though sometimes I think of the past and sometimes I see it
coming, catching up, hands caked with dried mud, head shaved clean.

PRAYER (SOMETIMES)

Maybe it's only waiting. Maybe you have
an idea: a glove dropped on the sidewalk

in the rain that has yet to be soiled, stepped
on, ruined. It sits gleaming, alone, useless

and forgotten, but beautiful, yellow (I think)
as a ripe banana, still warm inside. But if

that's your idea, then you're no longer waiting.
The condition of waiting is the way, just before

you pray, if you pray, the last thing you want
to do is pray, and the way the light might sit in

the window, taking you away from the prayer
and then, sometimes, right to the center

of the prayer. Maybe it's luck, or maybe it's
the condition of being lucky. It's not yours,

though it's in you, maybe, or maybe not. Either
way you'll never know it.

POEM AT THE END OF THE SCHOOL YEAR

I don't want to teach any more lessons to anyone, lessons I haven't
learned or lessons I have learned. I want to keep my lessons inside me.
I want to rise early and take my lessons for a walk in the brisk morning air
in a different state. I want to show them the mountains of my youth,
to be turned off by them at first but then marry them a few years later
in a simple ceremony surrounded by friends and family. *Need this?* I keep
writing in the margin of your poem. *More?* I keep asking your essay
about pollution, as if *More?* is a question your essay about pollution
can answer. Where the hell do I get off, anyway? Always with the better
idea, the advice, the pointing across a room to whatever it is I think
you need to be looking at.

DISCUSSING "THE FISH" THREE TIMES IN FOUR HOURS

Today I am a spoon among forks.
Yesterday I was a fork among knives.

Sometimes I am the knife.

In one class I am *What do you think this poem
is about?* and they are *What are we*

supposed to write? In the next I'm *Maybe
it doesn't matter what this poem is about,*

and they are *Why does she let the fish go?*
In the third class I am *Why does she let*

the fish go? and they are *What is this poem
about?* The glare of sun on the whiteboard

has nothing on the dry-erase marker and its
dangerous scent. I am *Tell me, what does your*

real life smell like? and they are *My life is really
none of your business.*

MY FATHER COMES TO GET ME

I've thrown up. The nurse has wrapped an ice pack in a brown paper towel, and I'm holding it against my forehead because that's what she told me to do. He comes right away in the clothes he wears to clean the bar, the sweat-stiff shirt he wears to mop the dance hall and stock the breathless coolers with beer, the cutoff jeans stained with tar. He comes right away and takes me into the shock-bright morning and puts me in the backseat and tells me to tell him if I feel like I'm going to throw up again. And then I go with him to do his life at eleven o'clock. At the cash-and-carry the man asks, *That your girl, Albert?* I have recovered enough to go in. How have I never been in this place before? Everything dusty, dimly lit, a man's place, a place for men. My father, standing in front of the enormous jars of maraschino cherries, takes one, then another, then, amazingly, another into his arms. *That's her,* he says.

THE BABY'S TOY

When the batteries
begin to die inside its white

plush belly, the assortment
of cheerful noises it makes

when you squeeze it
becomes singular

and crude, the sound
of a planet falling

through one universe
into the next, through

that one, too, falling
and falling into God knows

what, falling and falling
and never landing. Still,

the butterfly's face
(or whatever the hell

it's supposed to be—chirpy
bird? bumblebee?) stays

the same: knowing
smile, rosy cheeks.

PRAYER (BECOME A BUFFALO)

My husband and I have these conversations about moving
to the high desert mountains. Maybe eventually our conversations
will sprout saplings and what will begin as a pin on the horizon
will become a buffalo. Who cares if we ever move out of this house
with its fake wood floors and broken door in the bathroom?

My husband tries to help me with my prayers, but I do not pray
anymore and do not know how to pray, though I spend so much
of my time wishing I knew how to pray, which, I suppose, is very
close to praying, maybe as close as I'll ever get. Inside the body,
everything's real. Here are the baby's two fat feet dangling under
the kitchen table. Here is the baby holding one yellow spoon
while her father feeds her with another.

PRAYER (*NICE JOB*)

Today—everything in line, everything
done in an orderly fashion,
conversations with myself that end with
nice job—the baby sleeps and sleeps,

her big face composed, her eyes
brushstrokes, sweaty curls against her head.
I want my heart to belong to God, but
I can't help feeling that my heart belongs

to me. I want to give my heart to God,
but there isn't enough time. Or else
I want God to take my heart, to seize it.
Oh, how tiny I am in this heart. Today

is one of those days when I think
I could learn the names of all those birds
and plants, I could begin knitting
a gender-neutral blanket for Dalia's baby.

So I must look for it. Because that's
the only way to find it. Right? Where's
the cut? Where's this blood
coming from?

Carrie Fountain's poems have appeared in *The American Poetry Review, Poetry,* and *Tin House.* Her first collection, *Burn Lake,* was a winner of the 2009 National Poetry Series Award and was published by Penguin in 2010. She is writer-in-residence at St. Edward's University in Austin, Texas, where she lives with her husband, the playwright Kirk Lynn, and their children.

PENGUIN POETS